Siamese Cats

Jennifer Quasha

The Rosen Publishing Group's
PowerKids Press™
New York

For Keeks

Published in 2000 by The Rosen Publishing Group, Inc.
29 East 21st Street, New York, NY 10010

First Edition

Book Design: Michael de Guzman

Photo Credits: p. 1 © Richard Kolar/Animals Animals; pp. 4, 7 © Robert Maier/Animals Animals; p. 8 © Tetsu Yamazaki/International Stock; pp. 11, 22 © Reed/Williams/Animals Animals; p. 12 © Ken Ross/FPG International; pp. 15, 19 © Robert Pearcy/Animals Animals; p. 16 © Orion/International Stock; p. 20 © The Everett Collection.

Quasha, Jennifer.
    Siamese cats / by Jennifer Quasha.
        p.   cm. — (A kid's cat library)
    Includes index.
    Summary: Discusses the history, appearance, and behavior of this talkative cat breed, as well as its presence in contemporary American culture and homes.
    ISBN 0-8239-5509-5 (lib. bdg.)
    1. Siamese cat—Juvenile literature. [1. Siamese cat. 2. Cats.] I. Title. II. Series.
SF449.S5Q37 1998
636.8'25—dc21

                                                 98-46361
                                                  CIP
                                                      AC

Manufactured in the United States of America

Contents

This Siamese kitten will grow to be between six and twelve pounds.

The Siamese Cat

The Siamese cat is one of the most beautiful and **unusual**-looking of all cats. In fact, it is the most popular short-haired cat today. It has a strong **personality** and a **unique** appearance. The written history of the Siamese cat dates back to 1767, when it was first featured in an old book from Thailand called *Cat-Book Poems*. This book tells us that the Siamese cat is at least 200 years old. It is because of the Siamese cat's appearance and fun personality that it is still a favorite pet today.

A Land Called Siam

Siamese cats are originally from a country that was once called Siam. Today Siam is called Thailand. Thailand is on the continent of Asia. There is a **legend** that the king of Siam used Siamese cats to guard the **temples**. These cats would stand watch and warn the temple priests if they saw anyone coming. The people of Siam **adored** Siamese cats because they were so beautiful and they helped the king with a very important job.

Many years ago, in Siam, it was considered good luck to receive two Siamese cats as a gift. ▶

Pho and Mia

The first two Siamese cats to leave Siam were named Pho and Mia. Pho was a male. Mia was a female. In 1884, the king of Siam gave Pho and Mia to a British general. The general brought the cats back to England and gave them to his sister. The following year, she entered Pho and Mia in a cat show in England. Pho and Mia had cream-colored coats with brownish coloring on their faces, ears, paws, and tails. This coloring is called seal **point**. For many years after Pho and Mia arrived in England, seal points were the only Siamese cats that people wanted.

◄ *Pho and Mia would have looked just like these seal-point kittens.*

9

The Siamese Cat in America

Siamese cats were first brought to the United States around 1890. By 1900 the popularity of Siamese cats had spread all across the country. The first two Siamese cats to be shown in the United States were named Lockhaven Siam and Sally Ward. They were shown in Chicago, Illinois, at the Beresford Cat Show. This was the first cat show in the United States.

Though Americans love their Siamese cats as much as the king of Siam did, we don't use them to guard our temples and churches.

The Color of the Siamese Cat

The Siamese cat has a cream-colored body and darker coloring on its face, ears, paws, and tail. These are called points. There are four types of Siamese cats. These are seal point, chocolate point, blue point, and lilac point. When Siamese cats are born they are almost all white. As they grow older their colored points start to show. The points of a one-year-old cat will be much lighter than the points of a seven-year-old cat. The **temperature** of the air also affects their points. The colder it is where the cats live, the darker the cats' points will be.

◀ *This is what most people picture when they think of a Siamese cat.*

The Body of the Siamese Cat

The Siamese cat has a lean body with short hair and small, **delicate** paws. The coat of the Siamese cat lies close to its body, which is why it looks so skinny. It has a narrow head with a **triangular** face. Siamese cats have wide, pointed ears and a long, straight nose. All Siamese cats' eyes are blue.

The Siamese cat is known for its thin, sleek body. ▶

The cat has big almond-shaped eyes that slant in toward the nose. Sometimes the eyes are so slanted that the cat looks cross-eyed.

The Voice of the Siamese

The Siamese cat uses its voice more than any other cat. Some people say that their Siamese cats actually talk. A Siamese cat will meow and cry very loudly to get its owner's attention. It will meow when it is hungry and when it doesn't get its way. The Siamese cat's loud and unique voice has helped make this cat so popular.

This Siamese kitten will learn that the more it talks to its owner, the better chance it has of getting a treat.

Does the Siamese Cat Act Like a Dog?

Of all the **breeds** of cats, the Siamese cat can act most like a dog. Unlike most other types of cats, Siamese cats will come when you call them, and they can be trained to **fetch**. They make a lot of noise to get attention, just like dogs. Siamese cats will even beg for food. Very few other kinds of cats will do any of these dog-like things.

Siamese cats are one of the few breeds of cats that can be trained to do things. Some will even walk on a leash. ▶

Si and Am

Though Si and Am like to cause trouble, most Siamese cats just like to play. ▶

In Walt Disney's movie *Lady and the Tramp*, there are two Siamese cats named Si and Am. If you put Si and Am together they spell Siam. In *Lady and the Tramp*, Si and Am are full of **mischief**, just like real Siamese cats. In the movie, they try to get Lady and Tramp in trouble. In real life, Siamese cats usually don't want to cause trouble, they just like to have fun.

The Siamese Cat Today

The Siamese cat is the most popular shorthaired cat today. It is one of the easiest cats to recognize because of its beautiful and unique coloring. Though it has been a long time since the Siamese cat guarded temples in Siam, the breed has not changed very much since then. Today, all these years later, Siamese cats sit on our windowsills and use their loud voices to guard our houses.

Web Sites:

http://www.fanciers.com/
http://www.best.com/~sirlou/cat.shtml

Glossary

adore (uh-DOR) To love something very much.

breed (BREED) A group of animals that look very much alike and have the same kind of relatives.

delicate (DEH-lih-kit) Easily broken or hurt.

fetch (FECH) To go after something and then bring it back.

legend (LEH-jind) A story passed down through the years that many people believe.

mischief (MIS-chif) Trouble.

personality (PER-suh-NAL-ih-tee) How a person or animal acts and relates to others.

points (POYNTS) The different-colored face, ears, paws, and tail of the Siamese cat.

temperature (TEM-pruh-cher) How hot or cold something is.

temple (TEM-pul) A place where special religious ceremonies are held.

triangular (try-ANG-gyoo-ler) Shaped like a triangle.

unique (yoo-NEEK) One of a kind.

unusual (un-YOO-zhu-wul) Not common.

Index